The Jewish Child's First Book of Why

Alfred J. Kolatch
Illustrations by Harry Araten

 Jonathan David Publishers, Inc.
Middle Village, New York 11379

THE JEWISH CHILD'S
FIRST BOOK OF
WHY

Copyright © 1992 by Alfred J. Kolatch
Illustrations copyright © 1992 by Harry Araten

Jonathan David Publishers, Inc.
68-22 Eliot Avenue
Middle Village, New York 11379

10

Library of Congress Cataloging-in-Publication Data

Kolatch, Alfred J., 1916-
    The Jewish child's first book of why / Alfred J. Kolatch.
        p. cm.
    Summary: Presents thirty-two questions and answers relating to
Jewish holidays and customs.
    ISBN 0-8246-0354-0
    1. Judaism—Customs and practices—Juvenile literature. 2. Fasts
and feasts—Judaism—Juvenile literature. (1. Judaism—Customs and
practices. 2. Fasts and feasts—Judaism. 3. Questions and
answers.) I. Title.
BM700.K5923   1991
296.4—dc20   91-25352
                                                            CIP

Printed in Mexico.

Contents

- Why do we say "*Shalom*"?
- Why do we place a *mezuza* on the doorposts of our homes?
- Why is Saturday a very special day of the week?
- Why does Mother cover her eyes when she lights the Sabbath candles?
- Why do we eat *challa* on Shabbat?
- Why do we go to the synagogue to pray?
- Why is the Jewish New Year called Rosh Ha-shana?
- Why do we blow a *shofar* on Rosh Ha-shana?
- Why do we eat honey and other sweet foods on Rosh Ha-shana?
- Why do Jews fast on Yom Kippur?
- Why do we build a *sukka* before the holiday of Sukkot?
- Why, on Sukkot, do we say a special prayer while holding the *lulav* and *etrog*?
- Why do we sing and dance with the Torah on Simchat Torah?
- Why do we remember the Maccabees on Chanuka?
- Why do we light candles for eight nights on Chanuka?
- Why do we play with a *draydel* on Chanuka?
- Why do children plant trees on Tu Bi-Shvat?
- Why do we read the *Megilla* on Purim?
- Why do we eat *hamantaschen* on Purim?
- Why do we read the *Haggada* at the Passover *Seder*?
- Why do we eat *matza* instead of bread on Passover?
- Why do we celebrate Lag B'Omer?
- Why do we celebrate Shavuot?
- Why do we celebrate Israel Independence Day?

SHALOM שלום

Why do we say "*Shalom*"?

Shalom is a beautiful Hebrew word.

It is a word with many meanings.

It means "hello." It means "goodbye." And it means "peace."

When we meet a friend, we say "*Shalom*," and we mean, "Hello. Come in peace."

When we say farewell to a friend, once again we say "*Shalom*," and we mean, "Goodbye. Go in peace."

And when we pray for *shalom*, we hope that everyone in the world will live in peace.

שְׁמַע יִשְׂרָאֵל

Why do we place a *mezuza* on the doorposts of our homes?

A *mezuza* is placed on the doorposts of our homes to remind us that we are Jews.

The *mezuza* is a small container that holds a piece of special paper called parchment.

A few Hebrew sentences from the Bible are hand written on the parchment.

The first sentence is *Shema Yisroel, Adonai Elohenu, Adonai Echad.* In English, this means, "Hear O Israel, the Lord our God, the Lord is One."

The *Shema* reminds us how much God loves us and how He will make us happy if we lead good lives.

Why is Saturday a very special day of the week?

Saturday, the seventh day of the week, is Shabbat. *Shabbat* means "rest."

God created the world in six days, and on the seventh day He rested. We, too, rest on Shabbat after working all week long, and that is why the Sabbath is very special to us.

When we greet our family or friends on Shabbat, we say *"Shabbat Shalom,"* "Have a peaceful Sabbath!"

Why does mother cover her eyes when she lights the Sabbath candles?

Each Friday afternoon Mother prepares for Shabbat.

She places a beautiful white cloth and shiny silver candlesticks on the table.

Before it gets dark, Mother lights the Sabbath candles.

She then covers her eyes to help her think only about the beauty of the Sabbath and the words of the candlelighting blessing she is about to recite.

Why do we eat *challa* on Shabbat?

About 2,000 years ago, in the beautiful Temple in Jerusalem, twelve breads were placed on a special table and left there all week long for everybody to admire.

Each Friday, before the Sabbath, twelve fresh breads were brought out to replace the old ones. Each bread, which was called a *challa*, was considered holy.

Today, on the Sabbath, the holiest day of the week, we eat *challa* to remind us of the *challa* breads that were used by Jews in the Temple many years ago.

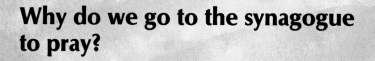

Why do we go to the synagogue to pray?

We can pray to God anywhere.

We can pray in our homes, in our backyards, or even in the woods.

But the best place to pray is in the synagogue, or temple.

We go to the synagogue because there we meet other Jews who have come to pray, and we feel good because we are together.

Why is the Jewish New Year called Rosh Ha-shana?

The Jewish New Year is called Rosh Ha-shana because in Hebrew *rosh* means "head" and *shana* means "year." Rosh Ha-shana is the "head" or "beginning" of the Jewish New Year.

We celebrate Rosh Ha-shana on the first day of the Hebrew month called Tishri. Tishri usually falls in the month of September.

SHOFAR

Why do we blow a *shofar* on Rosh Ha-shana?

On Rosh Ha-shana, we blow a *shofar* in the synagogue to announce that the new Jewish year is beginning.

A *shofar* is the horn of an animal. It may be the horn of a deer or antelope, but usually it is the horn of a ram.

The inside of the horn is hollowed out so that when we blow the *shofar,* beautiful sounds can pass through.

Why do we eat honey and other sweet foods on Rosh Ha-shana?

On Rosh Ha-shana, Mother makes sure to serve sweet-tasting foods.

Grapes, sliced apple, and other fruits of the season are placed on the dinner table next to a dish of honey.

Before eating the fruit, we dip it into the sweet honey and hope that we will enjoy a sweet New Year.

Why do Jews fast on Yom Kippur?

There is one holiday during the year when we spend the whole day praying in the synagogue. That holiday is Yom Kippur, or the Day of Atonement.

"Atonement" means saying we are sorry for the bad things we have done and promising not to repeat them. In our prayers, we ask to be forgiven for our mistakes.

To help us concentrate on the prayers we recite on Yom Kippur, we do not eat food or drink liquids throughout the day. Our thoughts are only on our prayers.

Boys of Bar Mitzva age and girls of Bat Mitzva age are expected to fast all day long. Younger children may fast part of the day if they wish.

Why do we build a *sukka* before the holiday of Sukkot?

Every year, five days after Yom Kippur, we celebrate Sukkot for a whole week.

Before Sukkot, we build a small hut in our yard or on our porch. The hut is called a *sukka*. It reminds us of the flimsy houses the Jews lived in while in the desert, after they escaped from Egypt.

We cover the roof of the *sukka* with branches and corn stalks. We hang fresh fruits and vegetables from the ceiling, and we dress up the walls with colorful drawings and decorations.

Many people eat their meals in the *sukka*, and some people even sleep there.

Why, on Sukkot, do we say a special prayer while holding the *lulav* and *etrog*?

Four different plants represent the harvest of the autumn season, the season when the Sukkot holiday is celebrated. A special blessing is recited over them every morning of the holiday, except on the Sabbath, to express our thanks for the food that comes from the earth.

The first plant of the four species is the *etrog*. It looks like a large lemon.

The second is the *lulav*. It is a tall palm branch.

To the *lulav* we attach a small holder with two pockets, and in the holder we place willow and myrtle branches. As we hold together the four types of plant life, we recite a blessing.

שִׂמְחַת תּוֹרָה

Why do we sing and dance with the Torah on Simchat Torah?

The Torah contains the first five books of the Bible. It takes one whole year to finish reading the Torah from beginning to end.

The day on which we read the last portion is called Simchat Torah, which means "being happy with the Torah."

To show how happy we are, we take all the other Torahs from the ark, and we parade with them around the synagogue. Children join the parade, carrying flags and waving them. Everyone sings and dances and has a wonderful time.

Why do we remember the Maccabees on Chanuka?

A long time ago there were five brave brothers called Maccabees.

They were called Maccabees because in Hebrew the word *maccabee* means "hammer." Each of the five brothers was very strong, like a hammer.

Brother Judah was the leader of the group. He was the strongest and bravest of all.

The Maccabees saved the Jewish people from the Syrians who ruled over Palestine 2,000 years ago. And every year, on Chanuka, we remember the Maccabees and their heroic deeds.

Why do we light candles for eight nights on Chanuka?

We light candles for eight nights on Chanuka to remind us of a great miracle that happened long ago.

When the Syrians ruled Palestine, they did not let the Jews practice their religion. They placed idols in the Temple in Jerusalem, and the *menora* that always burned in the Temple was put out.

After the Maccabees defeated the Syrians and chased them out of Jerusalem, the Jews wanted to light the Temple *menora* again. But all they were able to find was a small jug of pure oil—just enough to keep the *menora* burning for one day.

But, a miracle happened. The oil continued to burn for eight days!

And this is why we light candles on the eight nights of Chanuka.

DRAYDEL

סְבִיבוֹן

Why do we play with a *draydel* on Chanuka?

On Chanuka, we exchange gifts, eat potato pancakes called *latkes*, and play games with family and friends.

In one of the games, we use a *draydel*.

A *draydel* is a top with four sides. Each side has a different Hebrew letter on it: *nun, gimmel, hay*, and *shin*. These are the first letters of four words: *nes gadol ha'ya sham*, meaning "a great miracle happened there [in ancient Israel]."

The great miracle is that a little bit of oil kept burning in the Temple *menora* for eight days.

Why do children plant trees on Tu Bi-Shvat?

When the Hebrew month of Shvat arrives, winter will soon be over. The trees will start growing again, and all of nature will come alive.

The fifteenth day of Shvat, which we call Tu Bi-Shvat or Chamisha Asar Bi-Shvat, is celebrated as the New Year for Trees.

On this nature holiday, Jewish children all over the world go out into the fields and plant trees.

Why do we read the *Megilla* on Purim?

On Purim, in the synagogue, we read the scroll of Esther, which is called the *Megilla* in Hebrew.

The *Megilla* tell us that about 2,500 years ago, in ancient Persia (which today is called Iran), a beauty contest was held by King Ahasueros. The king's wife, Vashti, would not obey him, so the king decided to find someone else to be the queen.

The beauty contest was won by a girl named Esther (whose Hebrew name was Hadassah). When Esther became queen, she was able to save all the Jews of Persia.

Today, on Purim, young girls in many communities dress up in pretty costumes and enter a beauty contest just like the one in which Queen Esther participated many years ago.

Why do we eat *hamantaschen* on Purim?

In the Purim story, Haman was the wicked man who wanted to chase all the Jews out of Persia. Queen Esther and her cousin, Mordechai, were able to stop him.

On Purim, to remind us of Haman and his evil plan, we eat pastries made in the shape of a triangle, just like the hat Haman used to wear.

These tasty pastries, which we call *hamantaschen*, are usually filled with prunes or poppy seeds.

Why do we read the *Haggada* at the Passover *Seder*?

When winter is over, we know that soon we will celebrate Passover.

We all help clean the house very carefully to prepare for this beautiful holiday.

On Passover we hold a *Seder,* at which time we read the *Haggada.*

The *Haggada* is a book that tells the story of the first Passover and how the Jews escaped from Egypt and became a free people. We read the *Haggada* so that we will not forget this important event in Jewish history.

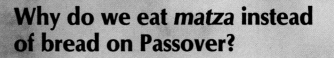

Why do we eat *matza* instead of bread on Passover?

On Passover, we eat *matza* instead of bread to remind us that when the Children of Israel were freed from slavery in Egypt, they had to leave in a hurry. The Egyptians were afraid that more plagues would befall them if the Israelites did not depart quickly.

So, the Israelites packed up their bread dough before it had time to rise. They took the dough along with their other belongings, and fled Egypt.

Later, when the Israelites baked the dough, the bread came out flat and looked like the *matza* we eat today.

Why do we celebrate Lag B'Omer?

Lag B'Omer is the thirty-third day after the beginning of Passover. There are many stories about why we celebrate this holiday.

One story is about a famous rabbi named Simeon who lived in the Land of Israel about 1,800 years ago. In order to avoid being captured by the Romans, the rabbi and his son hid in a cave for thirteen years. They ate only the fruit of the carob tree.

Each year, on Lag B'Omer, Rabbi Simeon's students would visit him. So that the Romans would not become suspicious of where they were going, the students dressed up as hunters, carrying bows and arrows.

When the students reached the rabbi's cave, they sang and danced and spent the night studying with their teacher.

In Israel today, on Lag B'Omer, children are free from school. They spend the day taking hikes, going on picnics, playing games, and singing around bonfires.

Why do we celebrate Shavuot?

Seven weeks after Passover, we are ready to celebrate the holiday of Shavuot.

Many years ago, in the springtime of the year, God gave the Ten Commandments to Moses on Mount Sinai. The Children of Israel waited at the foot of the mountain for Moses to come down with this precious gift.

As we celebrate Shavout in the spring of each year, we remember this special event in Jewish history.

Why do we celebrate Israel Independence Day?

In 1948, during the month of May, the Jewish State was established in the Land of Israel. Every year since then, on the Hebrew birthday of the new State, Jews in Israel and all over the world celebrate this joyous day by singing and dancing in the streets and holding huge parades.

The holiday is called *Yom Ha-atzma'ut* in Hebrew, which means Independence Day.

The Jews living in Israel today have come from more than fifty different countries, including India, Yemen, Iraq, Russia, Turkey, and Ethiopia. They all live together as one people.